Technology Skills for Kids

Building Your Technology Foundation:
"Know What You Are Using"

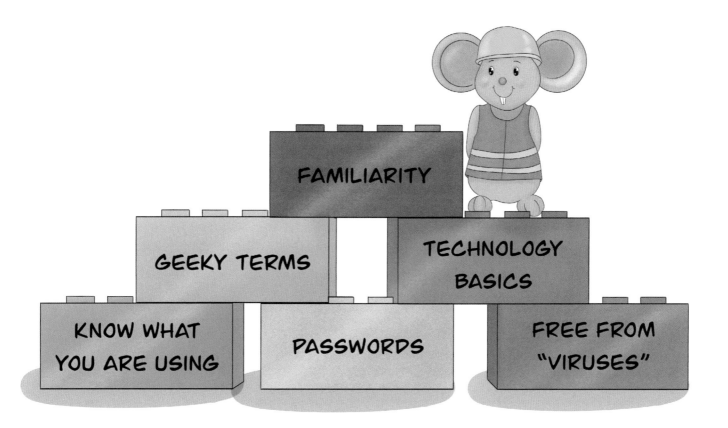

Hello and welcome!

This is **book #7** in a series of picture books created to help children make productive use of their computers and other devices while staying safe online.

Tough Cookie, Tech Wizard Mike & Tabby

Any words or phrases in **bold orange** are topics that will be explored further in this book's **supplemental materials**.

"Gosh, what _is_ this thing?"

1981 Flashback: Knowing what you are using has always been essential for methodical procedure.

A wizard and his tabby cat walk at night along a path. They see a poisonous snake barring their way and turn and run in the opposite direction.

As they return along the same path in the morning, they find a coiled rope on the ground.

If you need **help** with getting something done (e.g. creating a presentation), you will need to know what you are using.

You may need to positively identify any device you need to use in terms of its hardware and software.

Computer

Definition:

A <u>computer</u> is an <u>electronic machine</u> that
1) takes in data and instructions (input)
2) works with the data (processing)
3) puts out information (output)

Explanation:

<u>Computers</u> are made of HARDWARE
-input devices like the keyboard and mouse
- the CPU and memory
- stotage devices like hard drives
- output devisec like printers and monitors and SOFTWARE
(the instructions that tell the <u>computer</u> what to do)
- system software
- programs (application software)

The tablet and the stylus
(an input device) are hardware.

The app on the device used to create the
diagram on the screen is an example of
software.

It is very important to know which device you are using — including the operating system and the **version** of the operating system it is running.

All roads (or at least a good number of them) lead to Rome from having this info.

You need to know your device's operating system, which apps are suitable for a particular task or project and which file types you need to work with.

FILES

PROGRAMS

OPERATING SYSTEM

Speaking of file types, .exe files can install software onto a Windows computer.

Executable files can be good 😇 or evil 😈 so we need to be very careful with them. As always, if you are uncertain 🤨 about anything, get some good help.

An operating system (OS) is the program that manages all of the other application programs in a computer / tablet / smartphone.

You also need to know what you are working with in terms of cloud services...

Knowing what you are using in the technology world is just as important as knowing what you are using in the real world.

For example, the procedure to brew loose tea will be different than brewing tea bags (although the end result will be just the same).

In a nutshell, you should "Go CSI" on the device(s) that you are using for the purposes of getting stuff done, troubleshooting and getting good help.

Record your findings in your technology notebook.

Visual inspection

Look for a brand name and/or a logo on your device. And if you find one, record it and/or sketch it into your technology notebook.

Take notes and sketch ✍ This example device has a logo, a remote and ports. A visual analysis, a web search and/or a conversation might reveal its purpose(s).

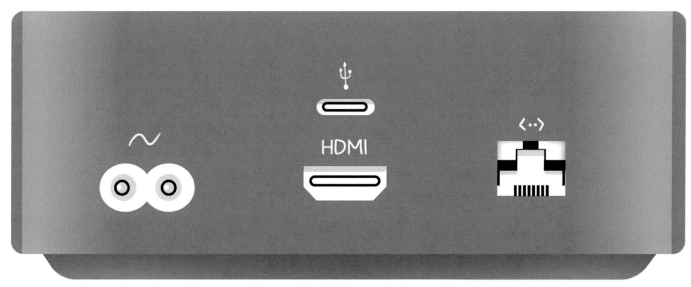

All roads lead to Rome (or at least a good number of them) from knowing what you are using.

A very simple definition of hardware is anything you can **physically touch** such as a monitor, a PC tower, a keyboard and a mouse…

Software includes your device's **operating system** and its various applications such as the messages app on a smartphone…

Well, bust my buttons!
—Doorman to the Emerald city

You should not "bust" the buttons on your device(s) but you may have to feel around for them. Press them and see what they do.

You can search the web for anything you need to know on any internet-connected device using a web browser app.

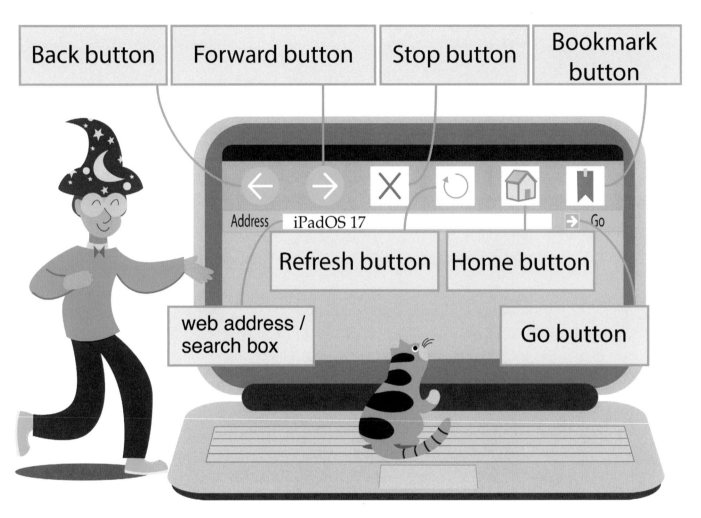

A device is basically defined by its operating system (e.g. Windows 11 and iPadOS 17).

Reminder: You may have to **noodle around** with any unfamiliar gadgets and/or applications to figure out their intended uses (but "**Bee Careful**").

If you do not know what something **is** (e.g. a particular app or device or peripheral or online service), you can search the web to learn more about it.

1. Formulate your search query.

2. Connect to the Internet (however that is done on your device. You may have to noodle around for that particular **functionality**).

3. Type what you are looking for (or what you would like to find out) into a **search box**.

Tabby Frisk   Navigation Transmutator

Web   Images   Maps   Shopping   More

About 192,000,000 results (0.18 seconds)

NAVIGATION TRANSMUTATOR - WHAT IS IT?
www.wizardandtabby.com/
Everything you want to know about Navgation Transmutator.

NAVIGATION TRANSMUTATOR - WEBSTER ONLINE
www.michupw.com/
Navigation is a field of study that focuses on the process of monitoring and controlling the ... Integrated Bridge System...

4. Peruse the search results page (you may have to scroll up and down and follow navigation breadcrumbs to find some good information).

If you want to know if a particular peripheral is **compatible** with your device, you can find out by searching the web.

A peripheral device is hardware that can be **connected** to a device (wirelessly or non-wirelessly) that provides additional functionality.

Examine your device for openings called "ports" — which enable you to **physically connect** peripherals to your device.

The number and types of ports vary widely between devices — and on this particular device, we also see an ethernet port which enables a **wired connection** to the Internet.

Knowing what you are using also extends to applications. You want to know which app you are using **and** if it is the app you should be using to accomplish a particular task.

A local cleric used a spreadsheet application to create his will and testament when he should have used a word processing application.

Knowing what you are using can enable you to seek out devices and/or applications that are more user friendly than what you are currently using.

User friendly

Easy to learn how to use.
Simple for people to use.

Not user friendly

User friendly

A device's "About" info is often found within its **Settings**.

The appearance of "About" screens will vary between devices but in general, you are looking for something like this:

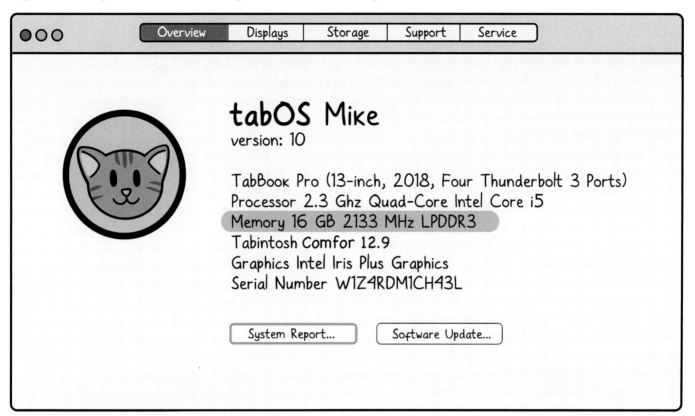

If your device is running slowly it could be because it does not have enough memory (highlighted above).

Carefully record into your technology notebook the information provided in your device's About Window

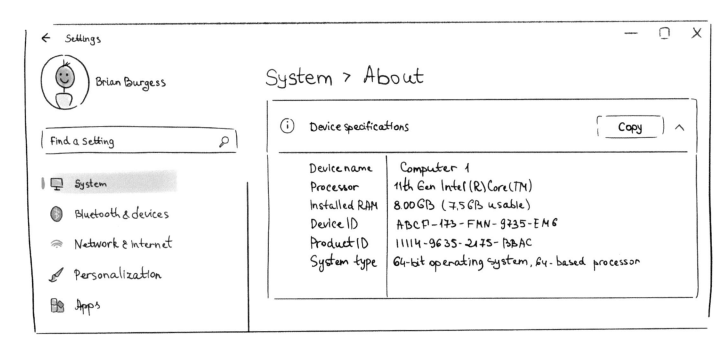

Don't be sad! Documentation will never go the way of the dodo.

Your device's model name and operating system will be especially important to record into your **technology notebook**.

This information is often essential for **getting good help** and **troubleshooting**.

Obsolete devices are very vulnerable to various forms of malware infection because they are no longer receiving security updates.

Rule of thumb: Devices that are over seven years old are obsolete.

You can **search the web for your device's release date** by its model name and/or serial number.

Knowing what you are using is very important — especially if you need to get some good help.

Tuffy is demonstrating his note-taking skills. Documentation will also serve you very well — especially when troubleshooting an issue with your device or one of its applications.

OBSERVATION VS INFERENCE

something fact-based you experience through one of your five senses

what you think or decide about something you have observed

Show an interest in what your friends are interested in. For example, Samantha loves antique VW Beetles.

"Politeness is an inexpensive way to make friends." — William Feather

Visit www.technologyskillsforkids.com for more tech skills for kids including blog posts, videos and **book #8** in which we continue our discussion of the technology foundation.